Approaching Poetry

poems by

Mark Grinyer

Finishing Line Press
Georgetown, Kentucky

Approaching Poetry

Copyright © 2017 by Mark Grinyer
ISBN 978-1-63534-347-2 First Edition
All rights reserved under International and Pan-American Copyright Conventions.
No part of this book may be reproduced in any manner whatsoever without written
permission from the publisher, except in the case of brief quotations embodied in critical
articles and reviews.

ACKNOWLEDGMENTS

I would like to thank the editors of the following publications, where versions of some of these poems have appeared previously either in print or on the Internet.

Mosaic: A Space with Words.
The Highlander: Ill Thinking of Keats; Stone City Roam; Poem in the Act of Becoming Nothing.
First Stone: Splash; Presence; Early Rising
Kansas Quarterly: In Satan's Place.
Cordite: Doll-Making.

Publisher: Leah Maines

Editor: Christen Kincaid

Cover Art: Mary Grinyer

Author Photo: Diana Grinyer

Cover Design: Elizabeth Maines McCleavy

Printed in the USA on acid-free paper.
Order online: www.finishinglinepress.com
　　　　　also available on amazon.com

      Author inquiries and mail orders:
        Finishing Line Press
         P. O. Box 1626
       Georgetown, Kentucky 40324
          U. S. A.

Table of Contents

Presence 1
In Praise of Sight 2
Early Rising 3
Approaching Poetry 4
Poem in Search of an Everyday Object 11
Manifesto 12
Je Est un Autre 14
After Chomsky 15
In Satan's Place 16
Reassembly 18
The Naturalist and the Mystic 19
On a Poem Left on the Moon 20
DNA: The Dance 21
Sometimes, Perhaps 24
Cosmology, Whole Cloth 25
Doll-Making 26
An Apology for Poems not Written 28
Page Poem 30
Cat Comments 31
Thanksgiving 32
Varieties of Snow 34
Poem in the Act of Becoming Nothing 35

Presence

I sit
as if in prayer,
with my hands folded,
and my mind crumpled
upon its restlessness;
with just this candle lit
before me as a flame.
I listen to the quiet.
It is not burning,
only there.

In Praise of Sight

Beyond that glass
the windblown trees;
inside, a candle shedding,
stilly, its trapped light.
Around that flame
no light is shed
on the museless focus of
his empty gazing into night.

Absorbed by night,
such smaller flames
burn stilly in closed rooms,
while there beyond
the window's glaze
light breezes stir
such shadows as
intensify the light.

In this, the smaller room,
mere movement sheds
on what there is
no greater praise than sight,
and some few words
that talk us through
these flickerings
of light and dark tonight.

Early Rising

Hailstones
drum spirits into morning.
They startle me awake;
and I recall the oldest
fear   the Present

Although I know
it is the graying of
the dawn, the rattle,
incessant in my ears,
assaults my windows—
and nothing else is clear.

Strange sounds, it seems,
and sights turn
mystic in the mind.
I touch the curtains. Yes,
I sneak the silken wait away
and look—

It is the greening of the dawn—
and sensing nothing different
say, "No spirit moves.
Prepare the dance of day."

Approaching Poetry

1.   A Modern Poem

Should be not
mean, contain
no ideas but

                In things, make
                a start out
                of particulars

                              Be but words
                              on a page spaced
                              into images of

                              Petals on a wet
              black bough bent
parsing the rain in

A re-visionary company.

2.   A Particular Tone

A particular tone
of this particular time
      and place it went
out like a lightning bolt, that poem
(one thousand one   one thousand two
one thousand three   one thousand four . . . .)
with rumblings like thunder.

And I confess, I could not scorn
              its sodden spiel nor fable.
Irregularity scants the breath
while sunshine stocks our table.

We smile . . . . some rictus
of the imagination.
Poem   Poem   Poem   Poem
Is that the beat?   If it is . . . Is it
Some *Zagat Guide*
       to illumination;

or is it the strain,
    the dulcet strain,
       the brilliant, streaming, sun-struck strain
of elimination?

          Shit!
The lights went out in this crazy world;
and our poets were
    unable.

3.   *A Poem Should Be Not Mean*

Chicken-tracked around the zig-zag page,
the first cracked egg pecked at the margins
timidly attempting flight toward song.

4.   *Splash*

To make a distance
   now, to penetrate
      the block
I'm looking in
   upon the figure now
    relax it,
       one unwilling muscle
           at a time.
It melts.
  The lower legs,
  the loins,
  the trunk and
      forelegs
      down to fingers
      deliquesce.

The head,   No
The head
   it will not follow.
How it leaps
      a lump of Ice out of
      the soup
turns

      upon its severed
              nods and stares
speaks with blood to ask
"What is this freak?"

This silence
    broken only by
            the splash.

5.   *Images*

They speak to me
who does not know you
as Plato's ideas speak
           to shadows
lost in time. Each image
           flickers
        TV-like
  in mind.

6.   *Ill, Thinking of Keats*

What sentences this
these coughings to get out
Some bolus of corruption, or
beneath that gluey slick
the purest adumbrations of
the self
         This all I get is air
not fragments of solidifying life

There are no pinkish
revelations in this phlegm
to culture in a Petri dish
no blooms of life
            For I
unlike John Keats
I have not caught
in this unfolding pettiness
the multitudinous measures of
the imagination's

        life.

7.   *Psycho Scriptor's Lines*

I—A TV scene—
stay up all night
      to write
or creep dark streets
  as cities sleep
     drinking
      in the dull-eyed lechery
        of porno houses, bookstores,
        bars and cheap hotels.
I populate those streets
 with restless versions
             stranded there
     of in-laws, mothers,
    wives, ex-lovers,
perfect sheep to
fill each sheet with,
sacrifice them there.

The butcher's bloody
             knife inside
             my God's will
keeps them
    stranded in
that unimpassioned
   glare.

8.   *Simile*

That's how
    you do it now,
just reach right out
   and grab
that simile
like
    a bird
    a tree.

9.   *At Play in the City*

With brother Rat I
scampered out through
that maziness in words
to doorways where I crouched
Beast-wise   Paralyzed
Between   Behind bare lines
I stunted there   and lied
      as I tricked out
         a woman
         a way across town
         a path
through billboard wastes
      Despised
Like music on a market street
The prize
    of rainbows hooked
      brought to net
      and fried
This language makes
    a tangle
Life defies

10.   *Stone City Roam*

It is
    there
        a poem.
You walk through streets
              of any poem,
of architectural grace
            touched down
            to cigarette butts
            and wads of gum
            stuck on concrete bones
                a stone
            city roam
fitting words struck hard against home.

11.   *A Space with Words*

I will not say,
                "It's beautiful,"
but it is quiet.
                The city tonight
speaks softly.
                It fills a space,
perhaps,
                with words, or
with blinking
                plastic lights.

12.   *Evening Lines*

So far
and in between
the words are gray
    In another tongue
They're all that is asked
        are the barrier, or
are just that smoke within
the cool skies of each

In each
they are the new moon
            invisible
As clouds between
        and shifting, are
these twenty-eight days
in cycles

Outside, we say
not even moonlight is pure
Inside, I say
we are the Andromeda strain

We hope we are
        beyond   of
              the stars above
A song.

13.   *Just for the Poem's Sake*

I would like to write
a poem just for the poem's sake
and not concern myself
with light.
I would like to sit awhile
                 tonight,
then break through these white walls into
some night bird's pure delight
     then pass it on in peace.

I would like to still the breath of time
as it drags cruel music
               from old lines
         forget the bitter stark refrain
of visions raised by desert heat
whose writhing makes them mine.

But ensorcelled here by words,
               intent upon the night,
I listen through these walls
      as birdsong calls young Icarus
to wing-beats like the breath of life
               resigned.

Poem in Search of an Everyday Object

The doorknob? No. The wall?
The TV set in front of books
on a wooden shelf
encased. In case of what?
In case some booby blows a tube,
or fol-de-rol, my threadbare clothes
turn furniture for cats.

I sip a scotch and think.
Think? Think everyday
is hardly worth a thought.
I drink. It'll put me sound
asleep tonight, I think,
for there's no pressure here
toward thought,
no images to act like cats
that jump up on my chest at night
to kneadle all the comfort from
my sloth.

I'm furniture, it seems,
a somewhat lumpy bed tonight
well tossed;
and I wish that fickle cat of mine
would stay outside tonight,
investigate the neighborhood,
get lost.

Manifesto

A poem is
What?
Is a poem . . .
Is . . .   Speak up!
     I can't hear you!
It may have . . .
Voices. Flexed
     for a moment in
     The din
The breath   Aloud in
Wind . . .   Songs
An interpretation
It may be . . .   On
the page   It
Dreams   It
Hangs on the screen
It may mean many things
     Simple things
     Or hard   but
A poem should be not . . .
I mean . . .   It
     Should move
Variously   Hesitant
Coming off the page
In rhythms   leafing out
From prose . . . It is   It
     Comments on itself?
What?   As it moves
     Wormish
Down the age
Chewing things—The leaves
     The trees
A poem is
As it must be . . . alive
     To day and night
     Intensity   Aware
     Of each but
Aimed at all   It
Cuts through these . . . Leaves

In a breath   It
              Is broken
Then   made whole.

Je Est un Autre

After G. Poulet

"*Je est un autre*" and
"*Je suis.*"
From a far field, I come
to poetry. A poem
here present on the couch,
presents itself
as my cat, Fred,
who twists beneath
my sloughed-off leather jacket,
attempting
to get comfortable within.

I am not Fred, I am
suspicious of his poise,
his will to find no words
no languages to speak,
just food and sleep,
and some slight warmth
and comfort in this skin.
They're all he needs,
it seems.

While I, I am not easy in
my skin. I walk
and talk beneath the weight
and fuzziness of words,
withdraw unrest with interest,
and pay back all this otherness
with wordplay and a grin.

I   is another   and
I am. Here I am
what drags weird words from Fred,
uncertain in his dreamful sleep—
this fantasy of being
something other than—I am,
instead of Fred, myself,
awake within this otherness,
not him.

After Chomsky

*"Colorless green ideas sleep
furiously"*

                Like wings of light, I say.
Depending on the point of view,
              the imagination applied,
this language doesn't hold.
But if we stand outside those wings,
            those particles or waves,
all color disappears—Like language then,
or thought   Colorless green ideas

Sleep furiously   When metaphors
              or speech that sings appears,
the letters on the page release
              some fury in the brain.
Like real or mythic wings aloft,
    or ambergris   reduced to gold
      redolent in a perfumed night
these sounds preserve a scented thought;
these words release a sign

A sign beyond the rough green sleep
              of ideas unapplied to life
Launching with great vigor
        into flight
            as meaning in the hearts of men
Where logic doesn't hold
       Semantics is winged victory
And colorless green ideas sleep
       furiously, in flames.

We need the light.
We need the heat and dreams.
Depending on the point of view
the sentencing applied,
each scent releases unfixed thought,
each sound announces time,
and colorless green ideas sleep
    furiously and fine.

In Satan's Place

for G. K.

What is this wet?
Your tongue—
detached from its place in your mouth
and placed, carefully, upon a page? A bait?
You speak good news;
of a family for once, apparently normal,
climbing the ladder of knocks,
looking for more;
of no disgrace.
But you never go back to fish.

And what is that step there, you missed,
the one you tripped over into telling—
telling your father (they liked your stuff)
what you missed, he missed;
your mother, what she missed;
telling your readers—myself—
what each of us,
each trout in the stream has missed,
and what we have gained.

What have we gained?
A beachhead in blood,
A ladder missing a rung?
A tongue, detached from its place
and placed tellingly—
like fish guts on a beach—
always and painfully telling me
about this space,
the missed connections that tear us apart—
like a railroad crossing the States—
like an ocean?

And what have we gained?
A father, a mother, a wife—
who do not understand, perhaps,
who will never understand,
how this tongue, held,
floating in the wet, wriggling,

detached from its place can speak,
coolly, like a poet at last,
of a heart, of all its hearts,
in a space, in private,
to an imagined few.

"The death of Satan
was a tragedy for the imagination."
Wallace Stevens, another fish
in an ocean of words, said that,
with impeccable manners and Harvard speech,
not those of your father, or mother, or wife.
He too was detached—like an island—
but now he's arisen,
a fish after bait into grace.

What then is this wet,
this loose-tongued clambering haste?
More Good News announced
in a stream to a few,
and then misplaced,
like an empty spot
we have crawled across
these states,
or the bathroom floor assault
of an infant seeking to taste his world
like a fish?
Once caught, we can never go back.

Reassembly

For John Bosley

Sometimes
when I think that I might be
just parts for someone else's body,
when evening stares me down,
and I am uneasy in this valley

Sometimes,
when this stillest colonnade of trunks
of arms leafed out in shades of green
and roots that go too deep to see
have closed all marches in, and I
am grown here voiceless in the valley.

Sometimes,
when I'm hung in places where
between the branches twisted grimaces and sky
these clouds of present shadow bite
a blank of broken daylight from God's eye.

Sometimes,
when in the iris of the sky we see
the darkness of those fading things on which
we stake our claim to heaven.

Sometimes,
when all our shaken senses say
that we must mark the parts "Returned,"
of someone else's body.

Sometimes,
something finds its voice,
and though it seems that we're unready,
we turn awakened bits of sense
into something new and worthy of
some new day's featured study.
Sometimes. . . .

The Naturalist and the Mystic

If the world is round
the stars are hot
the moon is a rock
and we are what
we know they're not
then nothing we say
can alter that

If the world is word
and that's a fact
and the moon is a disk
from where we're at
then stars are as small
as the world is flat

When what we see
as flat is flat
and what we are
is not just that
then nature's truths
are miraculous acts

And science seems
but lying tracts
ignoring all
that makes men great
some innate spark
that rises up

Toward unknown knowns
and crystal facts
undoing what we know is not

On a Poem Left on the Moon

> *"Do you need me*
> *I am there,"*
> James Dillet Freeman, "I am There"

And who I am is God; I am,
the invisible light;
the soundless voice;
the power in all hands, I am
the stillness in your life. No vision;
no inspiration matches this. The poem,

The only poem from earth that rests
with footprints on the moon
is a prayerful limping rhyme.
The *Esthetique du Mal* repeats
a more true tenor for our time.

This poem is too sure, I think,
to represent our history to time.
It neglects all those remnants
of insight found in pain,
in the sculptures of Dachau that stand,
with suicide vests and IEDs,
reminding us again
of many recent holocausts
and signs.

It fails to find truth's home again,
our crimes,
the wrongs made clearly visible
in Satan's face,
as seen in Milton's visions
from another brutal time,
the death unseen on TV screens,
behind those dim reflections
in the faceplates of our astronauts
as we fly the human race out
into space, into time.

DNA: The Dance

The genes read
        like a sentence,
              base by base,
        codon by codon,
a tract of triplex houses.
        How they twist around
              the street
    as the street twists
up and around another.
        It is the double helix,
            biologists say,
    of life,
a record of those traits,
        that once encoded
               out-lived death.

        Each home entails its base,
one of the four fixed
        molecules of life—
               of speech in threes
     whose grammar compels the shapes,
grown in place,
        that build a compound into codes
               for amino acids.
    The acids too,
like poetry compound
        after RNA,
               life's Mercury,
    code carrier,
transforms their words into acts,
        into cities around the earth,
               those factories in cells,
    the ribosomes in which,
if all goes well—
        the environment is right,
               the nutrients needed are
        abundant—
some proteins will be made,
        specifically,
               which if we live

                    are the masterworks,
          the tangled integrations of
                    our lives.

                         One might well think
               this code laid bare
     in the crystal clarity of sentences,
               of sense and nonsense there,
                         of mis-sense when mis-stated,
               mutilated, by broken bonds,
     makes whole the act of living,
               truths the night,
                         the city of the cell within the state,
               the process of
     the chemistry of life.
               But such metaphoric flights,
                         such fancies in the night,
               transform the din
     of accident into
               harmonious flights,
                         poems of the world in which
          we believe we must believe,
     those certitudes of right
               on which we act in life,
                         insisting that,
               as each street twists up
     and twines
               around another
                         and living chaos shrinks,
               our truth is right,
     the only light with which
               we can parse the night
                         until those proteins break
          into fragmentary bits
     and neighborhoods decay
               into slum-bound tenements
                         where warring tribes fight
               as cells dividing might
     with other cells,
               turn treacherous and kill.

                    There,
            our unborn children fail,
grow legless, armless,
            fall senselessly to smash,
                        like earthquake shaken
            architecture,
helpless in the dance.

Sometimes, Perhaps

Sometimes,
when what we want within
     is to hear them chattering again,
And what we want to do
     is to go wandering through
        poetic rhapsodies drawn
           from figments now long gone
like some forgotten blues song.

Sometimes,
when all there is, is songs
     and singing fails our home
leaving riots in the streets
     and years of weak retreats
         from justice in the heat
of our indifference and mistakes,
  our ignorance, and that fall from grace
which brought us to this barren place in time.

Perhaps then, we ask,
        Does poetry proceed
           from screams
           from intense speech
              drawn
     from God knows what
     desperate passions
     and the need
for justice in the streets.

Perhaps then, we think
       that this won't last beyond
          that moment when
        we bite the dust, and
      our verbal intent fades
     into another era's
fear and rage.

Cosmology, Whole Cloth

For Carl Sagan, and prophets everywhere

Some, it's small,
        insensate warp in fabric twists
                these strands above
the bedded plane
   on which old prophecies prevail

        Beneath that surface, where
sheer light-
        lessness prevents
                all coarse attempts at color
      Black holes await—
and realms behind,
        beyond black holes—the threshold of
eternity, perhaps,   The start
                of the big bang,
a point of night without time or space,
containing all that is, or ever will be.

We have studied it; let it suck
                long thoughts
from minds that otherwise might be
                too delicate and sterile. But
                too often now, it seems,
We're caught in this waste
        of the warp and woof of history
           through which new versions of
                the universe may fall,
                        may fold into
                the rudeness
        of antipathies left
          by weavers in
                  the patterns
of multi-colored yarns.

Doll-Making

After Vonnegut

She sits before the TV screen
and needles russet comedy from cloth.
While the re-run witch
talks through her laugh
and zap, unravels time and space,
she fades into the ad biz of the age.
A million bony fingers stuff gray fluff
into her carapace of cloth,
but the fabric of her mind
is much too rough;
the slightest touch
unravels it from thought.

While our interstices bleed
ice-nine into the cradle of
her life; while the digits
of our thought embroider time
and curlicues of space
onto the skinship of her mirth;
and while we laugh,
say "so it goes" until we drop;
the grinning lips of comedy uncurl,
until just beyond the blackest,
vacant snuffles of pure sloth,
before we rise,
before the up-turn of a smile;
she stops,
and crowns that yarny head
with a cherry colored fools-cap
and a laugh.

Such actions speak much louder here
than words;
the ends of empty stitchery,
they lift us from this fantasy,
and short commercial blurbs
to leave us with her memory,
unraveling epiphanies of trash—

and that is when,
sewn carefully to cloth,
her scarlet velvet heart
leaps out to us.

An Apology for Poems not Written

I have, it's certain here,
    now scanted much
        of much more interest
        to this atomic age
than lacks of lust,
    peculiarly, to know
        what's crawling in, or out,
        between our legs.

No shy pornographer, you say,
        should bow his way away
        from the clear content of his age;
from his body's speech,
    his future's shape
nor from the message on the media's wide stage.

But since, of course, we are, we know,
        mere naked apes
    here playing out
        our consciousness and rage,
and since, of course, it's plain to us
        that in our nakedness all interest is ingrained

In brains, the race is run,
        now here in words, now there in space,
and sometimes, in between us,
        with a gun,
and we know nothing but
    new trouble's kingdom come.

The trouble is, of course,
        the seep and spurt of love.
    It is, it isn't purely made, but
        compounded from old ironies and crimes.
And if we were, or weren't,
    some transmutation here to try,
and from this clear atomic principle, to scry,

A need for firmer stuff, less free,
    mere stasis would set in,
        no change,

and change is life,
we say—no way.
We cannot be, in poetry, so free.

Page Poem

The page is blank.
What forces it to fill
with fake details
from weak shadows
on some pale Platonic wall
in light above this keyboard where
these words have been abstracted
from musings growing stale.
as I type them into ASCI code
inside the laptop's shell,
reworking lines and saving them
in records full of evidence
that old ideals imperiled
have fallen to faint signatures
as incomplete and frail
as pixels flashed at 60 Hertz
by key strokes into software faking
pages onto desktops built
in languages abstracted
from Google spaced adventures
as inspiration fails.

We've fallen from great truths
once known, now lost to us, it seems,
in readouts on glass walls.
These legacies gone missing might
bring peace to those who struggle with
complexities in these machines
the emptiness of glowing screens
replacing human contact with
a glutton's world of data
without context or control
flashing letters onto LEDs,
but hiding local truths derived
from living here and now
in a world built by people finding
worth in what they do,
in histories of living with
what thinking people feel

Cat Comments

I crumple up canary bond
and toss it to my favorite cat
who bats it back and forth
across the lawn.

The gray-backed beast of dawn
she makes no critic's sense of this
but throws her big-eyed self about
to capture these, my windy flights, for fun.

In street lights on a summer night,
a demiurge of sight, I think,
she pounces on the mothwings
of a song.

She holds it in extended claws
my gutted inspirations torn
like broken bits of gypsy moth,
soon gone.

Thanksgiving

1.
Watching
the dawn come
into the house from
night

After reading
Williams all
night.

The trees appear,
the tree—
an American strain

Hump of roots
right angle to trunk

The fluted
red-brown ridges
of bark up
to the first branch

Bare almost
of needles
five inches long
in fountains of three

Burnt
but alive where
one large prickly cone dropped,
Heavy with seed

Planting the duff
of last year's burning.

2.
After dawn breaks,
the composition
brilliant under sunlight
opens

The fire's down,
but still we await
the birth
of another day with
its golden calf.

It is too early yet
to make the passing
of twelve more hours
into memories,

But interrupted
now and then
by pops
and disintegrating crackles,

We understand
that there are things
we must do.

Go to the bush.
Choose
two branches and

Kindling
place them on
the coals—

To wake and watch
the burning.

Varieties of Snow

These words are snow
in wind   as are the white
petals fallen   A drift
from trees   in spring

Awakenings   for all to see
of summer's green days
    The flutterings
    of snow-winged butterflies
    against the edge of shadows
        under which I walk

As I look up   and see
    in the fall sun's glare
White   as light made soft
    a sift of down floating   down
of cottonwood seeds aloft
And these are also snow

As dropped
like flakes of ice
    on singing wings
        The waking up
    of dour winter calls
    The crystal snow
of time home
        to all.

Poem in the Act of Becoming Nothing

Infinitude.
The Universe.
The Milky Way; one sun.
The act of light transforming sky
to blue. Green lifted out of dawn,
a dozen scattered laurels hold
one iridescent starling's voice
up chittering from dew.

Inscaping still, stillborn,
the wish that could transform that voice,
as transient as fresh dew at dawn
to light airs fraught with sun.
Words bend intent
towards worlds reduced,
then gravitate
to gone.

An early Baby Boomer, **Mark Grinyer** was born into a military family in Colorado Springs, Colorado. His first 14 years were spent as a military brat, moving with his family from city to city, around the country and around the world. This ended in 1960, when his father retired from the Air Force and moved the family to Riverside, California. He went to high school and college there, and graduated with a BA in English from the University of California, Riverside in 1968. After serving in the Army during the Vietnam conflict, he returned to the University to complete his graduate education. There, he immersed himself in graduate school, in teaching and in the extra-curricular opportunities presented by his participation and leadership in the poetry scene on campus. He wrote his PhD dissertation on the early poetry of William Carlos Williams.

After briefly testing the educational job market in 1980, he decided to try a career as a technical editor, writer, proposal development specialist and manager in industry. This career choice offered him the opportunity to make a decent, stable and enjoyable living for 27 years, during which, while he continued writing poetry, he made few attempts to publish it. In 2006, he retired from industry and returned to teaching. He taught Business Communication at California State University, Fullerton for the next two years, and then returned to work in industry, working for a year and half in Texas before returning to Southern California, where he continued working on proposals until 2011 when he retired.

Since the late 1960's, he has published poems in a variety of print and internet journals around the country and overseas. These include *Green's Magazine, The Kansas Quarterly, The Literary Review, The Pacific Review, The Spoon River Quarterly, Perigee, Cordite*, and others. *Approaching Poetry* is his first chapbook publication. He is also seeking publishers for several additional books of poems.

www.ingramcontent.com/pod-product-compliance
Lightning Source LLC
LaVergne TN
LVHW041551070426
835507LV00011B/1048